How to Write a University Level Paper in 7 Days

The Quick Guide to Writing Research Papers, Article Summaries, and other assignments

by

Ronald W. Stephenson II, Ed.D.

Cassandra A. Stephenson, M.Ed.
Editor

2017

Text copyright © 2017 Ronald W. Stephenson II
All Rights Reserved

Dedication

This quick guide is dedicated to the student who is up at 5:00 am putting the final touches on a research paper that is due at 8:30 am. If this is you, grab another cup of coffee and read on!

About Me and this Quick Guide

My name is Dr. Ronald W. Stephenson II and I have been an adjunct professor at Wilmington University for over 8 years. I have also earned a Bachelor's, two Master's, and a Doctoral Degree. During my day job, I am a teacher of students with autism.

I have written numerous university level assignments (including a dissertation) and graded even more. This book is a quick reference on how to write for college. If possible I suggest you divide your writing into the days I described, if not try to adhere to the described schedule as much as possible. Many of the steps for the Research Paper, Article Summary, and other assignment are the same, sometimes with small differences. Just like with your papers, don't procrastinate, start reading.

Introduction

- This quick guide is for the college student who wants to improve their writing.
- This guide and the examples provided within will help with
  - grammar
  - mechanics
  - writing and word usage
  - APA citations
  - general university level paper formatting
- This book will provide step by step instructions on how to write university level papers.
- The first 8 Chapters and the Appendix serves as the quick guide. The other three Chapters, Chapter 9, 10, and 11 provide an example of an APA literature review with an annotated bibliography.

Writing is not only important in college but in society in general. Before a person gets to know you, your writing is often the only way that you will be evaluated.

Copying

Feel free to copy parts of this book and use it as a checklist. The Appendix is designed for this purpose.

Disclaimer

This book is only my opinion; this book does not represent the views of Wilmington University or any other institution of higher learning. Additionally, the use of these techniques does not guarantee improved grades.

Table of Contents

Chapter 1: How to Write Research Papers

Day 1: **Choose** a topic that you are interested in (if possible). The more your interest, the more you will write, and the more often you will write. Then thoroughly read the **assignment directions** and the **rubric**. Make sure your topic fits, if you have questions ask your professor.

Day 2: **Search** the Library, EBSCO Host, Google Scholar, and Google in addition to other sources of information. Make sure you save the name and site where you obtained your articles (so you can quickly go back to them in case they get lost or your computer freezes). *Even if you do not re-write an author's information word for word, an in-text citation and corresponding Reference page citation is required.* **Always back up your work!**

Day 3: **Briefly** read the articles or other information to make sure that they will fit into your paper. With the articles and information that fit, make sure you create the appropriate corresponding citation (APA or MLA). It is much better to do this now and get it out of the way instead of waiting until the end; I know this from experience.

Day 4: **Outline**, divide your topic into an introduction, at least three subtopics, and a conclusion. Then document which article should go with which section of your paper.

Day 5: **Start Writing**, pay close attention to what information was obtained from what source. Highlight information that is not your own and keep it highlighted until you have created the appropriate in text citation. Do not write your conclusion now. If possible, read your entire paper, then write your conclusion. This way your paper will be fresh in your mind and you will be ready to summarize/ conclude.

Day 6: Depending on how much you have already written, **continue** to write or **reread** and **proofread** your paper and then write your conclusion. After your conclusion is finished, have your entire paper proofread by a reliable person.

Day 7: **Correspond** with your proofreader, make changes, reread your paper and then submit.

Chapter 2: How to Write Article Summaries

Day 1: **Read** the Article, yes read the entire article.

Day 2: **Read** the **assignment directions** and the **rubric**. Highlight the assignment directions in various colors. Copy the entire article and paste it onto a Microsoft Word Document. ***Make sure you properly cite the article***. Place the required citation (APA/ MLA, or other) at the top of your word document. **Always make sure you provide proper credit to your sources**. *You are only transferring the author's words onto a Word document so you can highlight them in the various colors that Word provides*. As you read the article again highlight the various sections in the color that correspond with the assignment directions that you will be answering with the information highlighted. **Never** write an author's words directly into your paper unless you provide the proper citation as a direct quote (author, year of publication, page, paragraph, or section number). Remember, directly quoting an author's information is fine as long as you provide the proper citations and you do this sparingly. *Even if you do not re-write an author's information word for word, an in-text citation and corresponding Reference page citation is required.* **Always back up your work!**

Day 3: **Outline** by dividing your topic into an introduction, at least three subtopics, and a conclusion. Then document which piece of information should go with which section of your paper.

Day 4: **Read the Rubric again,** then start writing, pay close attention to what information was obtained from what source. Highlight information that is not your own (I use yellow for this) and keep it highlighted until you have created the appropriate in text citation. Do not write your conclusion now. If possible, read your entire paper, then write your conclusion. This way your paper will be fresh in your mind and you will be ready to summarize/ conclude.

Day 5: Depending on how much you have already written, **continue** to write or **reread** and **proofread** your paper and then write your conclusion. After your conclusion is finished, have your entire paper proofread by a reliable person.

Day 6: **Correspond** with your proofreader, make changes, reread your paper and then submit.

Chapter 3: How to Write Other University Level Assignments

Day 1: **Read** the assignment directions and the rubric. Highlight the assignment directions in various colors. If possible, copy the information required for your assignment and paste it onto a Microsoft Word Document. Make sure you properly cite the information. Place the required citation at the top of your Word document. ***Always make sure you provide proper credit to your sources.* You are only transferring the author's words onto a Word document so you can highlight them in the various colors that Word provides.** As you read the information again, highlight the various sections in the color that correspond with the assignment directions/ rubric sections that you will be answering with the information highlighted. **Never** write an author's words directly into your paper unless you provide the proper citation as a direct quote (author, year of publication, page, paragraph, or section number). Remember, directly quoting an author's information is fine as long as you provide the proper citations and you do this sparingly.

Day 2: **Briefly re-read** the information that needs to be included within your paper. With this information, make sure you create the appropriate corresponding (APA/MLA or other) citation. It is much better to do this now and get it out of the way instead of waiting until the end; I know this from experience. *Even if you do not re-write an author's information word for word, an in-*

text citation and corresponding Reference page citation is required. **Always back up your work!**

Day 3: **Outline** by dividing your topic into an introduction, at least three subtopics, and a conclusion. Then document which article should go with which section of your paper.

Day 4: **Start writing**, make sure you pay close attention as to what information was obtained from what source. Highlight information that is not your own and keep it highlighted until you have created the appropriate in text citation. Do not write your conclusion now. If possible, read your entire paper, then write your conclusion. This way your paper will be fresh in your mind and you will be ready to summarize/ conclude.

Day 5: Depending on how much you have already written, **continue** to write or **reread** and **proofread** your paper and then write your conclusion. After your conclusion is finished, have your entire paper proofread by a reliable person.

Day 6: **Correspond** with your proofreader, make changes, reread your paper and then submit.

Chapter 4: What Professor Stephenson looks for (sentences like this that end with a preposition!)

Do not generalize when writing your papers, "everybody knows…"

The reality is everybody does not know, and if they did, we (myself included) cannot possibly know this.

Grammar

There were significant grammatical errors (fragmented sentences, run on or confusing sentences, subject-verb disagreement, ill-formed verbs, pronoun errors, possessive errors, extra, wrong or missing words).

<u>Writing Style and Word Usage</u>

The writing was unclear, incoherent, and not concise. Opinion was provided throughout the paper. The writing was unorganized, and difficult to read. The thoughts were disorganized and not developed in a logical sequence. There were significant mistakes in writing style and word usage (repetition of words, inappropriate words/phrases, too many short sentences, imprecise vocabulary, non-professional vocabulary, missing introduction, missing conclusion).

<u>Mechanics</u>

There were significant mechanics mistakes (spelling, capitalization, punctuation, fused words, compound words, duplicates, abbreviations).

<u>APA</u>

There were errors in APA formatting (e.g., font style, font size, font color, appropriate margins, the first sentence of a paragraph should be indented, double spacing, cover and reference page, etc...).

> *<u>Note:</u> Even though a paper may have excellent content, grammar, writing style and word usage, mechanics, and APA formatting mistakes detract not only from your grade, but your credibility as well.*

Chapter 5: APA (See your respective manuals, including the APA 6th edition. This APA list is not all-inclusive, please review the APA 6th edition for a complete list of all the APA rules.)

1. Technically, in APA, every time you utilize an outside source there should be an in-text citation; however, this tends to look messy. Additionally, one in text citation at the end of your paragraph is unclear and may be confusing, leaving the reader guessing regarding where your information was obtained. Best practice is to start with the citation (you can

use different varieties of in-text citations, examples can be found in Chapters 10 and 11) and end with an in-text citation.

2. All information that was obtained from another source is required to be cited with both an in-text citation and a corresponding source on your reference page, failure to comply with this is plagiarism.

3. Your "Running head" should also be written in Times New Roman.

4. Your "Running head" should be written in all capital letters.

    a. Running head: THIS BOOK IS INFORMATIVE

5. Your "Running head" title should be written in all capital letters on every page.

6. The words "Running head" are not written in all capital letters and should only appear on your cover page.

7. The "Running head" on the cover page and on your subsequent pages is a shortened version of your title

    a. Title - THIS BOOK IS INFORMATIVE

    b. Cover Page - Running head: THIS BOOK IS

    c. Subsequent Pages - THIS BOOK IS

8. The first sentence of a paragraph should be indented.

9. Your entire paper should be written in 12-point font.

10. Your entire paper should be written in Times New Roman.

11. Your entire paper should be written in black font (even the reference page, there should not be hyperlinks).

12. Double spacing is required throughout your paper.

13. If a quote is more than 40 words, treat as a block quote. Indent and no quotation marks.

14. If you quote a source *word for word* you are required to provide a page number or in the case of information from a website a section or paragraph number.

15. Avoid contractions in an APA formatted paper.

16. APA suggests using two spaces after periods.

17. Spell out any number used to begin a sentence

18. Only end sentences with one period after the citation.

19. Paragraphs should be at least 3-5 sentences long.

20. With the title of your sources on your reference page only the first word, word after a colon, and proper nouns are capitalized.

21. With your reference page, only books and journals are italicized.

22. When there is no author for a web page, use the title and include quotation marks around the title, example ("APA Sixth Edition," 2016).

<u>*Note*</u>: *Failure to cite correctly is technically considered plagiarism.*

Chapter 6: General Writing Tips

➢ Have all your papers proofread by your school (if they offer this service) or a reliable proofreader (like my mom, a retired teacher).

➢ Review the assignment directions **and** the assignment's rubric while writing your papers.

➢ Make sure you explicitly follow each and every rubric dimension.

➢ Ask a question about an assignment before the assignment is due.

➢ At the very least, read the assignment's directions and rubric once you receive the assignment.

➢ Use your textbook (if this is allowed), your textbook is an *excellent* source of information and you paid an *excellent* amount of money for the book.

➤ If an assignment calls for a certain number of pages, do not just add "fluff" at the end to make your paper longer. Also, do not add extra spacing between paragraphs to make it longer. Include substantial information, not "fluff."

➤ Do not write the way you talk, this is college. Certain words and phrases do not have a place in college papers.

➤ I am sure you heard this one before, DO NOT PROCRASTINATE!

Note: Write concisely, if the rubric states a certain number of pages and if you run out of topic to write about, do not just add "fluff." Dig deep, research, and find interesting and worthwhile information to write about.

Chapter 7: Recommendations

- I suggest you use one of your old papers that was formatted correctly as a template for formatting. Be careful with this though, just because one professor accepts your formatting does not mean it is correct or that another professor will accept the formatting.

- Self-Plagiarism – Self plagiarism is not a myth, if you use information from previous papers, just cite yourself (correctly of course). I used to think, how can my professor possibly know if I used this paper before. Well, with tools like *Safe Assign*, papers are uploaded into a database and the papers are compared to other papers within the database. Each upload adds to the database. In other words, your professor will find out.

- When I wrote my papers, I used the paper's assignment directions and rubric as a checklist to make sure that I included all the required elements. I also used the ~~cross-out font~~ to keep track of what information I already included within my assignment. Once I knew (or thought I knew) that I completed an aspect of the assignment directions or rubric ~~I simply crossed it out~~.

- Red & Blue Squiggly Lines – Do not make our job as professors too easy. When I grade a student's paper and see squiggly lines, that means the student should see (and correct) the grammar and spelling error before they submit their paper to me. Red and blue squiggly lines are Microsoft Word's way to inform the writer that they *may* have made a mistake. Sometimes Word will red squiggly line someone's name and consider it misspelled, conversely Word does not catch every mistake. Microsoft Word's self-checking feature is an excellent place to start your proofreading.

Note: If you can see the red and blue lines, so can your professor.

Chapter 8: More Tips from Professor Stephenson

- ✓ On your reference page, make sure that each source is listed. With the title of your sources on your reference page only the first word, word after a colon, and proper nouns are capitalized (sentence case).
- ✓ "Based off," it should be based on, "start off," how about just start, the off is an extra word (unnecessary). Also, this book itself is a great read. The word "itself" is extra and unnecessary. This book closed out with an Afterword. The word "out" is unnecessary.
- ✓ Ampersands (&) are used within in text citations, for example (Stephenson & Anderson, 2017) correct, *(Stephenson and Anderson, 2017) incorrect.* Ampersands are also used on your reference page when you are writing your authors' names.

✓ No quotation marks on your reference page

✓ Possessive errors, years! Very rarely are *years'* possessive. Back in the 1970's is incorrect. The year 1970 is not possessive. Back in the 1970s is correct.

✓ Words like big, done, and huge should not be used in university level papers, more precise and professional words should be used. Utilize the synonym feature in Microsoft Word or an online thesaurus.

✓ Any title within your paper, including subtitles should be capitalized (with the exception of the articles {a, and & the} and certain pronouns depending on your title).

✓ In a list of words, the last word before the "and" needs to have a comma following the word. For example, my favorite sports are hockey, MMA, and football.

✓ Be careful with "it's" and its. It's should not be used since it is a contraction.

✓ Watch out for, their, there, and they're. The last one should not be used since it is a contraction.

Note: Think of it this way, the Reference Page lets the reader know that you used someone else's information (which is fine) the in-text citations lets the reader know where within your paper the outside information was used. Without in-text citations I am unsure what information is yours and what information is not yours.

Chapter 9: Explanation of the Literature Review with an Annotated Bibliography (next Chapter)

A Literature Review is research paper that details what research has taken place before. In other words, what the experts have to say about your topic. An Annotated Bibliography is basically a reference page with a great deal of extras. The Annotated Bibliography provides details on the articles you are using for your research. The negative aspect of writing an

Annotated Bibliography is that it is more work. The positive aspect is that once it is written, the writer can easily find and use information from the various articles contained within the Annotated Bibliography. I suggest using Annotated Bibliographies especially when you are researching various studies or any type of information that may be difficult or has many different sections. An example is provided in the next chapter.

I wrote the following Literature Review with an Annotated Bibliography in 2011, during my second doctoral class. As you can probably imagine from reading the following paper, that second doctoral class was challenging (I wanted to use the word "hard" here; however challenging is more precise and sounds more like a university term). Please keep in mind that the example does not have a Running head. The Running head on the cover page and the subsequent pages are as follows (do not forget, your Running head is a shortened version of your title):

Title - What a Professor Wears Has an Impact on Student Perceptions

Cover Page - Running head: WHAT A PROFESSOR WEARS

Subsequent Pages - WHAT A PROFESSOR WEARS

With the cover page and subsequent pages, the "Running head" should be a shorter version of your title.

Chapter 10: An Example of an APA Literature Review with an Annotated Bibliography

(with comments and explanations)

- Please keep in mind that the following paper was written in APA 6th edition format.

- See your respective manuals, including the APA 6th edition. The following examples will not cover every aspect of APA (for instance, no abstract was required for this assignment). Please review the APA 6th edition for complete information regarding all the APA rules.

  [Explanation details are written in 10-point, Comic Sans, italicized font, surrounded by brackets within sentences (usually after commas), after sentences (after periods), and after paragraphs.]

What a Professor Wears Has an Impact on Student Perceptions

Ronald W. Stephenson II

Wilmington University

What a Professor Wears Has an Impact on Student Perceptions

Introduction

Does a professor's attire have an impact on students' perceptions of their instructor? Ten conclusions can be inferred about a person based exclusively on their attire: "economic level, educational level, trustworthiness, social position, level of sophistication, economic background, social background, educational background, level of success, and moral character" according to Thourlby (1978) (as cited in Lavin, Davies, & Carr, 2009, p. 2). *[The information in quotation marks was written in Thourlby's 1978 publication and I obtained this information on page 2 of Lavin, Davies, & Carr's 2009 publication. Et al. (and others) will be used in subsequent citations of (Lavin, Davies & Carr 2009) since there are three or more authors, when there are three, four, or five authors used the first time an in-text citation is written, write all the authors' names, during subsequent in-text citations use et al. When there are six or more authors, use et al. each time, even during your first in-text citation.]* College students may be creating the same conclusions about their professors. If students are generating the same conclusions, this could have an impact on how they perform in class, perceive their professor, and ultimately how students rate their professor on the often-used teacher rating scales. *[Notice the comma before the "and." When there are three or more phrases and the second to last phrase receives a comma before the "and."]* Teacher rating scales are used both formatively and summatively. In the formative sense, these evaluations can help an instructor improve his teaching style and methodology. As a summative tool, the teacher rating scales are used by college administration and may "provide information relevant to promotion, tenure, and pay decisions" (Carr, Davies & Lavin, 2009, p. 52). *[The information in quotation marks was written on page 52 of Carr, Davies & Lavin's 2009 publication. Keep in mind that the information cited earlier in this paragraph was from a different publication. Even though the names of the authors and the year is the same, it can be distinguished from the previous citation from the order in which the author' names are written. Authors' names are written by order of contribution, the first author contributed more, the second author not as much and so on.]* Consequently, a professor's attire could indirectly effect personnel decisions. Additionally, clothing "influences four kinds of judgments, including credibility, likeability, interpersonal attractiveness, and dominance, and thus serves as a primary impression management tool" as reported by Molloy (1975, 1977) (as cited in Lavin, Carr & Davies, 2009, p. 95). *[This information was written by Molloy in a 1975 and a 1977 publication, I obtained the information on page 95 from Lavin, Carr & Davies' 2009 publication. On your reference page, you will only cite the secondary source or the source that you read. In this case, the secondary source or the source I read was the Lavin, Carr & Davies' 2009 publication.]* College students may be making these judgments based on an instructor's clothing; if this is the case a professor's attire could have an impact on college instructors' careers. *[This information came from me; therefore, a citation is not necessary. However, if I developed this sentence on my own and I already used it in a paper I wrote back in 2011, I would be required to cite myself (Stephenson, 2011).]*

Organization

This paper includes the following headings: Introduction, Background, Definitions of Attire, Prior Research, Present Research, Conclusion, References, and an Annotated Bibliography. The Introduction is divided into the subheadings: Organization and Inclusion Criteria; Background, which is split into Business World and College Classroom; and the Present

Research section is separated into Purpose, Sample, Procedure, Findings, Limitations, and Further Research. *[No citation required, this is an original sentence, here I am just describing how this paper is organized.]*

Search Strategy and Inclusion Criteria

The search used for this literature review included EBSCOHost and Google Scholar. The key words were 'correlation between students' perception of their professor and their final grade,' this search resulted in few accessible peer-reviewed articles, as a result the search was revised into 'student perceptions of their professor's attire.' Within EBSCOHost the following databases were used: Academic Search Premier, Business Source Complete, CINAHL with Full Text, Communication & Mass Media Complete, Computers & Applied Sciences Complete, Education Research Complete, ERIC, Funk & Wagnalls New World Encyclopedia, GreenFILE, Health Source: Nursing/Academic Edition, Humanities International Complete, Library Information Science & Technology Abstracts, MasterFILE Premier, MEDLINE, Middle Search Plus, Primary Search, PsycARTICLES, PsycBOOKS, PsycINFO, Regional Business News, SocINDEX with Full Text, AgeLine, Mental Measurements Yearbook with Tests in Print, and eBook Collection (EBSCOhost). *[This sentence is my own, no citation required, this sentence explained how I obtained the information for this assignment.]*

Background

Business World

Among American organizations, casual dress in the workplace is routine, companies such as IBM and the Ford Motor Company allow casual attire on a daily basis (Sebastian & Bristow, 2008). *[This is not a direct quote; however, the information was obtained from Sebastian and Bristow's 2008 publication, I just put their information into my own words. As a result, Sebastian and Bristow get the credit.]* In the business world, there are many perceived advantages of

employees wearing casual clothing. These advantages can be characterized into two domains

financial and social. From a financial standpoint, employees save money on the purchase of

formal business attire and the elimination of dry-cleaning expenses. Socially, "communication

barricades" between leadership and 'general' workers are sometimes lifted as the result of both

parties dressing casually (Franz & Norton, 2001, p. 79). *[This information was obtained from a*

Franz and Norton 2001 publication and appeared as it is written within quotation marks (direct

quote) on page 79. Additionally, the preceding sentences (the sentences after the last in-text

citation) were all derived from information from Franz and Norton's 2001 publication; however, they

were not directly quoted.] Casual dress policies are often viewed as a reward or incentive in

many organizations by employees. According to the admittedly "limited survey evidence,"

casual dress policies in the workplace will lead to improved employee performance (Franz &

Norton, 2001, p. 81). *[In this sentence the words "limited survey evidence" were directly quoted*

from Franz and Norton's 2001 publication and was found on page 81, the rest of the information is

also from the Franz and Norton 2001 publication but was not directly quoted.]

Contrary to the aforementioned information, there is a negative aspect to casual dress in

the workplace. Research based on the correlation between people and how they perceive

themselves indicates that a person's attire affects their self-perception. *[The information from the*

first two sentences and the information in the next sentence before the comma was originated

from Rafaeli, Dutton, Harquail, and Mackie-Lewis 's 1997 publication and I found it in Franz and

Norton's 2001 publication, the citation for these sentences is located in my next sentence.]

People not only "define their roles" by their choice of clothing as reported by Rafaeli, Dutton,

Harquail, and Mackie-Lewis (1997) (as cited in Franz & Norton, 2001, p. 81), they also perceive the attributes of their occupation based on the way they dress according to Kwon (1994b) (as cited in Franz & Norton, 2001. *[The information in this sentence after the comma originated from Kwon's 1994 publication and I found it in Franz and Norton's 2001 publication. The 'b' after 1994 is present because Franz and Norton must have already used one of Kwon's 1994 publications ('a'), the lower-case letter after a year within a citation represents more than one citation by that particular author or group of authors in the same year.]* Even though casual dress may have a positive effect on employee attitudes, it could have a detrimental effect on employee performance (Franz & Norton, 2001). *[This information was obtained from Franz and Norton's 2001 publication; a page number is not required since this is not a direct quote (not word for word).]* Another argument against casual dress in the workplace suggests that employees wearing "formal dress strongly affects how people are treated and that formal codes on dress improve performance, motivation, and attendance" as stated by Molloy (1988) (as cited in Sebastian & Bristow, 2008, p. 196). *[This information originated from Molly's 1998 publication and I found it in Sebastian and Bristow's 2008 publication on page 196.]* Additionally, "other writers have suggested that increasing informality is among the causes of the decline in civility of the workplace, where casualness becomes chaos" according to Gonthier (2002) (as cited in Sebastian & Bristow, 2008 p. 197). *[This information originated from Gonthier's 2002 publication and I found it in Sebastian and Bristow's 2008 publication on page 197.]*

College Classroom

According to Lavin, Carr, and Davies (2009) higher education faculty, possibly more than other occupations have substantial discretion regarding their work attire. As a result, what instructors wear at different and the same institutions can vary greatly. What a professor wears is important since college instructors are often perceived as role models to their students. *[The information in these three sentences was obtained from Lavin, Carr, and Davies' 2009 publication.*

Please note that order of authors is important. Even though the publication in the block quote

below has the same authors and same year as the information obtained in the sentences above, it is

a different publication.]

> Professors
>
> may be serving as an example of what is or is not appropriate in terms of behavior and
>
> appearance. Likewise, the extent and even reach of the professor's influence as a
>
> knowledge source and mentor may, perhaps, be dependent upon what he wears or at least
>
> by how her attire is perceived. (Carr, Davies & Lavin, 2009a, p. 4)

[The information in the two sentences above represents a block quote. A direct quote of 40

words or more starts on a new line, is indented and the in-text citation is written after the

punctuation. Page, paragraph, or section numbers are also included as with direct quotes of

less than 40 words. I placed an 'a' after 2009 in the in-text citation since I used more than

one of Carr, Davies, and Lavin's (in that order) 2009 publications within my paper.]

According to Sebastian and Bristow (2008) to students who attend college full time and

do not hold jobs, their professors may be one of the few 'professional adult' role models that

these students interact with on a regular basis. Aspects of a professor's, demeanor, overall

attitude, and attire may provide messages to students. Subsequently, many college students

today have full time or part time employment and make the transition from college to the

workplace on a day-to-day basis. They may be receiving conflicting messages from work and

school; "these students often face either organizational formality or organizational informality"

(Sebastian & Bristow, 2008, p. 197). *[All the information in this paragraph was obtained from*

Sebastian and Bristow's 2008 publication, the information within quotation marks (the direct quote) was from page 197. A good way to make sure your reader understands that all the information in one paragraph is from the same source is to start your first sentence with a citation, in this case, "According to Sebastian and Bristow (2008) ..." and end your last sentence with a citation from the same source.]

In higher education, many believe that a professor's principal obligation is to ensure that students "become active participants in their own learning" (Lavin et al., 2009, pp. 93-94). *[Here et al. (and others) is used since there are three or more authors, when there are three, four, or five authors used the first time an in-text citation is written, write all the authors' names, during subsequent in-text citations use et al. When there are six or more authors, use et al. each time, even during your first in-text citation. The pp. 93-94 was written within the direct quote since the directly quoted information was obtained from two pages within the Lavin et al. 2009 publication.]* Factors such as appearance may influence a student's desire to learn (Carr et al., 2009a). *[Et al. is used since there are three authors and I already used this citation.]* According to Chickering and Gamson (1987) "learning is not a spectator sport. Students do not learn much just sitting in classes listening to teachers, memorizing pre-packaged assignments, and spitting out answers. They must talk about what they are learning, write about it, relate it to past experiences, and apply it to their daily lives. They must make what they learn part of themselves" (p. 1). *[The information in these three sentences was obtained from Chickering and Gamson's 1987 publication. According to Chickering and Gamerson (1987) is just a variation of an in-text citation, remember when 'and' is written in a sentence spell the word, in a parenthetical citation use an ampersand (&). Also, I placed the page number at the end since the three sentences ended with a direct quote, since I started with a citation and ended with a page number, a reader should realize that all the information was obtained from the same source, in this case Chickering and Gamson's 1987 publication.]*

Researchers have proposed that students consider the "following nine characteristics, listed in order of importance" traits of an effective college level educator: "(1) student-centered; (2) knowledgeable about the subject matter; (3) professional; (4) enthusiastic about teaching; (5) effective at communication; (6) accessible; (7) competent at instruction; (8) fair and respectful; and (9) provider of adequate performance feedback described by Witcher et al. (2003), (as cited in Carr et al., 2009a, p. 42). *[This information was from the Witcher et al. 2003 publication and I found it in the Carr et al. 2009 publication on page 42. The 'a' is utilized after 2009 since I used another Carr et al. 2009 publication in my paper and the page number is utilized since I am quoted word for word.]* In addition to a professor's attire being related to the overall perception of 'professionalism' that they convey to their students, an instructor's manner of dress correlates with their student's perception of their professor's knowledge and competency. *[This information is my own, these are some thoughts I had as an adjunct professor who wears jeans and colorful T-shirts to class. As you can tell, in a research paper, the vast majority of information is obtained elsewhere, there is very little room for opinions, maybe in your conclusion.]*

Definitions of Attire

Recent research defines formal attire for males and females as a "business suit" (Lightsone, Francis & Kocum, 2011, p. 21) or "suits with pants" (Lightsone et al., 2011, p. 18). *[Here I have two separate citations even though the information was obtained from the same source, this is because I used two direct quotes from the same source, but from two different pages (21 and 18).]* Semi-formal for the females consisted of a " black shirt dress with leggings and the male in Khakis and a white T-shirt under a blazer" (Lightsone, et al., 2011, p. 18). *[This information is from the Lightsone et al., 2011 publication on page 18.]* Casual dress as a T-shirt and jeans for females and shorts, "a T-shirt, and open long-sleeved button-down shirt for male faculty" (Lightsone, et al., 2011, p. 21). *[This information is from the Lightsone et al. 2011 publication on page 21.]*

Prior Research

In past studies, it was found that formal attire enhanced "student perceptions of their" instructors' "credibility, intelligence and competence, but" diminished "observed perceptions of likeability and approachability" according to Leathers (1992) (as cited in Lavin et al., 2009, p. 95). *[This information was obtained from the Lavin et al. 2009 publication on page 95, Lavin et al. obtained the information from Leathers' 1992 publication.]* Other studies have concluded that professors who "dressed formally were viewed as being more organized, knowledgeable, and better prepared. While those wearing less formal clothing were seen as friendlier, flexible, sympathetic, fair, and enthusiastic" as reported by Rollman (1980) (as cited in Lavin, et al., 2009, p. 95). *[This information was obtained from the Lavin et al. 2009 publication on page 95, Lavin et al. obtained the information from Rollman's 1980 publication.]* Prior research has also established that student learning is positively affected by the perceived credibility of the instructor according to Thweatt and McCroskey (1998) (as cited in Lavin, et al., 2009). *[This information was obtained from the Lavin et al. 2009 publication, Lavin et al. obtained the information from Thweatt and McCroskey's 1998 publication.]* "Students also tend to recommend credible instructors to others" Nadler and Nadler (2001) reported (as cited in Carr, Lavin & Davies, 2009, p. 52), *[This information was obtained from Carr, Lavin and Davies' 2009 on page 52, Carr, Lavin, and Davies obtained the information from Nadler and Nadler's 2001 publication.]* "respect them," stated Martinez-Egger and Powers (2002) (as cited in Carr, et al., 2009, p. 52), *[This information was obtained from the Carr et al. 2009 publication on page 52, Carr et al.*

obtained the information from Martinez-Egger and Powers' 2002 publication.] "and evaluate them

highly" according to Teven and McCroskey (1997) (as cited in Carr et al., 2009, p. 52). *[This*

information was obtained from the Carr et al. 2009 publication on page 52, Carr et al. obtained the

information from Teven and McCroskey's 1997 publication.] Carr et al. (2009) and Sebastian and

Bristow (2008) discovered that students ascribe more expertise to instructors who are formally

dressed as compared to their casually dressed peers. Consequently, formally dressed professors

were rated lower regarding likeability (Carr et al., 2009; Sebastian & Bristow, 2008). *[Two of my*

sources had this information so I gave them both credit, the Carr et al. 2009 and Sebastian and

Bristow's 2008 publication. Notice that I started the first sentence with a citation and ended the

second sentence with a citation, this was to ensure that the reader understands that the

information in both sentences was obtained from the two sources. Additionally, notice that in the

in-text citation both sources are listed with a semicolon in between. Furthermore, the order in

which the two citations are listed are not important, just alphabetical (the order in which they will

be listed on your reference page).]

Prior research has also established a possible gender bias, it seems as though students

may display "same gender preferences in their perceptions" of college instructors (Lavin et al.,

2009, p. 105). *[This information was obtained from the Lavin et al. 2009 publication on page 105.]*

It was also established that regarding teacher ratings "female students gave higher ratings" than

"did male students" reported Basow and Howe (1982) and Ferber and Huber (1975) (as cited in

Carr, Davies, & Lavin 2009b, p.3) *[This information was obtained from Carr, Davies, and Lavin*

2009's publication on page 3 (the 'b' signifies the second Carr, Davies, and Lavin's 2009 publication

that I used. Furthermore, Carr, Davies, and Lavin obtained the information from two sources,

Basow and Howe's 1982 and Ferber and Huber's 1975 publication.] and "that male students generally gave female instructors lower ratings as compared to male faculty" described by Basow and Silberg, (1987) (as cited in Carr et al., 2009b, p.3). *[I obtained this information from the Carr et al. 2009 publication on page 3, Carr et al. obtained the information from Basow and Silberg's 1987 publication.]* "In contrast, male student evaluations did not vary according to the gender of the instructor, but female students gave instructors of their own gender higher ratings as compared to male teachers" according to Bachen et al. (1999) (as cited in Carr et al., 2009b, p.3). *[This information was obtained from the Carr et al. 2009 publication on page 3, Carr et al. obtained the information from the Bachen et al. 1999 publication.]*

Present Research

Purpose

The purpose of the studies was to determine how professors' clothing effects student perceptions about a professor's credibility and professionalism (Lavin, et al., 2009). *[This information was obtained from the Lavin et al. 2009 publication.]* The general hypothesis among the studies was that formal attire would lead to enhanced perceptions of expertise and credibility with decreased perceptions of likeability and openness (Lightstone, et al., 2011; Sebastian & Bristow, 2008). *[I obtained this information from Lightstone's 2011 and Sebastian and Bristow's 2008 publication (two sources).]* There were a few variations regarding gender within the studies; the studies researched were mainly exploring both male and female instructor's attire with two exceptions. Carr et al., (2009) examined the perceptions of females only while Carr et al., (2009b) was limited to male professors. *[Here I discuss information obtained from two different (but similar sounding) publications, both written by Carr et al. in 2009.]*

Samples. Non-random, purposeful, voluntary sampling was employed with the studies explored. Non-random and purposeful since specific college classes were identified and the sample was voluntary since as previously discussed within the "Procedure" section, the completion of the survey was optional. *[No citation required, here I am just discussing aspects of this paper.]* For the most part, the studies' participants were business students from mid-sized Midwestern universities with the exception being the Lightstone, et al. (2011) research that was conducted at a Canadian university. *[Here I am discussing specific information (the participants) about the Lightstone et al. 2011 study, as a result I cited Lightstone; even though I am discussing specific information on a page (paragraph or section) number is not necessary since I did not document any information word for word.]* The Lightstone, et al. (2011) research was also the exception regarding the major of the participants, this study included business as well as psychology students. *[Again, I am discussing Lightstone's 2011 publication, therefore I included a citation.]* Additionally, the Carr et al. (2009b) study included "MBA and MPA (Master of Professional Accountancy) programs" and "several undergraduate mass communication, political science," "psychology classes," and "two first year law school courses" (p. 5). *[The majority of this sentence is a direct quote (words surrounded by quotation marks, the other words are mine; however, all the information was obtained from Carr et al.), here I started with Carr et al. (2009b) and ended with the page number where I found the information, this is just a variation of an in-text citation for a direct quote.]* The mean number of participants in the studies was 388 and the median was 450. The fewest participants were 103 while the largest number was 506. *[The information from these last two sentences was the result of a calculation that I created from the studies I used for my research. I did not use an in-text citation since the reader can determine where I obtained the information from reading the sentence, "mean number of participants in the studies…"]*

The gender of the participants was discussed in two of the studies; Sebastian and

Bristow's (2008) and Carr, Davies, and Lavin's (2010) study. *[Here I simply documented the two studies that I am discussing.]* In Sebastian and Bristow's (2008) research, there were "103 students (43 women and 60 men)" in the first study and "154 students (82 women and 72 men) who participated in the second study" (p. 198). *[Most of this sentence is a direct quote, here I started with Sebastian and Bristow (2008) and ended with the page number where I found the information.]* In the Carr et al. (2010) study, participants "were fairly evenly split between female and male, with 216 (47.6%) female respondents and 237 (52.2%) male respondents" (p. 51). *[Again, most of this sentence is a direct quote, here I started with Carr et al. (2010) and ended with the page number where I found the information.]*

Procedures. In three out of the seven studies, participants were provided with photographs of faculty members dressed in various forms of clothing while the remaining studies provided written descriptions of the professor's attire being examined. *[This sentence describes aspects of my paper and is an overview of information I found in the various studies that I used.]* The participants were then asked questions about each faculty member via a written survey (Lavin et al., 2009). *[This information was obtained from the Lavin et al. 2009 publication.]* One of the studies contained an on-line aspect that did not differentiate from the "traditional" survey except in its delivery mode (Lightstone et al., 2011). *[This information was obtained from the Lightstone et al. 2011 publication.]* The only other difference (however slight) in survey delivery that was noted within the studies was Sebastian and Bristow (2008) "who seated the participants" in a theater style room that contained a large screen projection system and folding desks for writing (p. 198). *[This sentence contains a direct quote from Sebastian and Bristow's 2008 publication and was obtained from page 198.]* It can be inferred that the other studies that were "traditional" in delivery were administered in college classrooms. *[This sentence is from me and* *describes broad aspects of my paper.]*

All the studies reviewed were quantitative and cross-sectional in nature. *[This sentence is also from me and describes broad aspects of my paper.]* Students answered the questions by providing a numerical value to their answers as exemplified in the Lavin et al. (2009) research. Respondents ranked how "a professor's attire would impact their perception of the instructor, where 1 = significantly positive, 2 = somewhat positive, 3 = no difference, 4 = somewhat negative, and 5 = significantly negative" (p. 6). *[The information in these sentences was obtained from the Lavin et al. 2009 publication, the information in quotation marks was obtained from Lavin et al. 2009 on page 6.]* As mentioned previously, the lone difference was Sebastian and Bristow (2008) who employed a choice between adjectives. *[Here I simply discussed Sebastian and Bristow's (2008) publication.]* Furthermore, data were collected at one point in time. *[This sentence may sound funny, but it is accurate, the word data is plural.]*

Two different versions of a study were utilized in three of the studies researched. *[This sentence is my own.]* With the Lavin et al. (2009) study two different versions of their survey were used "to change the order in which the" (p. 98) photographs of the instructor's "clothing was presented. In one case the instructor was depicted wearing casual, business casual, and professional dress (Version 1) respectively, while in the second version the same instructor was depicted wearing professional, business casual and casual clothing (Version 2)" (p. 98). *[With the preceding two sentences, I started the first sentence with a part of my in-text citation, in this case the author and year; and I ended the last sentence with the page number where I obtained the direct quote. I placed the (p. 98) after the first part of the direct quote just to ensure that the reader understand this information also was obtained from page 98. I would rather provide too much information regarding my sources than too little. Basically, this is just a variation of an in-*

text citation for a direct quote. Keep in mind that the direct quote is only 39 words; therefore, it is not a block quote.] In Sebastian & Bristow's (2008) research two surveys were used although it was unclear the reason for this. This research was not only examining the impact of instructors' attire on student perceptions but also the impact of instructor's form of address on student perceptions of their professor. The additional survey may have focused primarily on the forms of address aspect of the research. *[With these sentences, I am just discussing aspects of Sebastian & Bristow's (2008) research.]* In the Carr et al. (2009a) research two different versions of their study were employed as well; "one version asked students to assume the professor's attire and appearance was professional while the alternative assumed unprofessional dress" (p. 7). *[I started the sentence with the author and year of publication portion of my in-text citation and ended with the page number portion of an in-text citation for a direct quote.]*

Another variation of the procedure in which the studies were implemented was Sebastian & Bristow's (2008) research where there was a screen in front of the classroom and participants were instructed to view a description of the instructor that corresponded with the photograph the respondents were viewing. Additionally, this survey asked the participants to "rate the stimulus persons on 18 trait adjective pairs" (p. 198). *[The information in these two sentences was obtained from Sebastian and Bristow's 2008 study, the second sentence ended with a direct quote from the same Sebastian and Bristow publication.]* This research

> used the 15-item scale developed by Ohanian (1990) to measure the attractiveness (unattractive or attractive, not classy or classy, ugly or beautiful, plain or elegant, not sexy or sexy), trustworthiness (undependable or dependable, dishonest or honest, unreliable or reliable, insincere or sincere, untrustworthy or trustworthy), and expertise (not an expert or expert, inexperienced or experienced, unknowledgeable or

knowledgeable, unqualified or qualified, unskilled or skilled). (Sebastian & Bristow, 2008, p. 198)

[This is a block quote, a direct quote of 40 words or more, if you highlight a block of text Microsoft Word will count it, in this case there are 64 words in this quotation. Indent as you would a new paragraph, start a new line, no quotation marks, and the citation is placed after the final punctuation.]

The other studies examined asked questions such as:

The level of the instructors' preparation for class.

The instructor's knowledge of the material (i.e., subject matter).

The instructor's ability to present information clearly and in an understandable manner.

The student's overall evaluation of the instructor.

The reputation of the institution.

The value of the educational experience. (Lavin, et al., 2009, p. 98).

[This is a block quote of 47 words, indent as you would a new paragraph, start a new line, no quotation marks, and the citation is placed after the final punctuation.]

Regarding the studies where questions were asked, half of these studies included questions that were divided into categories while the other studies consisted of a single list of questions. *[This sentence is my own, here I am describing an overview of the studies that I used within my paper.]* The categories of questions amongst the studies were "how the instructor's attire would influence their overall appreciation for the course," "how the professor's appearance would impact their own engagement in the classroom," and "how the professor's appearance might affect their own engagement outside the classroom" (Carr, et al., 2009, p. 43). *[This information was obtained from the Carr et al. 2009 publication on page 43, it is a series of direct quotes.]* Other categories were "Instructor Characteristics that May Impact Credibility," "Instructor Credibility," "Student Effort and Behavior" (Lavin, et al., 2010, p. 54) *[This information was obtained from the Lavin et al. 2010 publication on page 54]* "credibility, character, and likeability measures" (Lightstone, et al., 2011, p. 19). *[This information was obtained from the Lightstone et al. 2011 publication on page 19.]* The aforementioned questions and categories of questions were referring to either a photograph or a written description of instructors dressed in formal, semi-formal, or in casual attire. *[This sentence was written to provide clarity for my previous sentences, it is my own, no citation required.]* Many of the questions were influenced by existing evaluations at the researchers' institution (Lavin et al., 2009). *[The idea for the sentence did not come from me, instead it came from the Lavin et al. 2009 publication.]*

A consistent theme throughout the studies was that the participants were informed that the professors' manner of dress was a personal preference and factors such as: "classroom conditions (e.g., heating, cooling and ventilation), the class setting (e.g., evening class, length of class session), delivery mode (e.g., face to face versus distance) and his or her individual preferences and comfort" (Carr et al., 2009b, p. 4) should be taken into account. *[The directly quoted information within this sentence was obtained from the second "b" Carr et al. 2009 publication that I used, on page 4. The portions of this sentence that are not directly quoted are from me. A reader should be able to infer this given the nature of the sentence.]* Additionally, students were notified that the studies were not intended to be an appraisal of any specific instructor and formal dress codes did not exist at the colleges where the studies took place (Carr et al., 2010). *[This information was obtained from the Carr et al. 2010 study.]* It can be inferred that all the participants of the studies examined were informed that the surveys were optional and the results confidential. *[This sentence is my own creation, no citation required.]* One study included an extra credit incentive for its participants (Lightstone, et al., 2011). *[This information was obtained from the Lightstone et al. 2011 study.]* Another theme throughout the studies was the participants reporting of their demographic information. *[This sentence describes an overview of the studies, no specific information from any individual study was used.]*

Findings. Professors wearing formal attire were perceived as being "more credible" (Lightstone, et. al., 2011, p. 7) *[The information in this section of the sentence was acquired from the Lightstone et al. 2011 publication.]* and formal attire "led to greater attributions of expertise than did casual dress" (Sebastian & Bristow, 2008, p. 200). *[This is a direct quote obtained from Sebastian and Bristow's 2008 publication on page 200.]* Conversely, formal attire was perceived as a weakness in regards to an "instructor's willingness to answer questions and listen to student opinions" (Lavin et al., 2009 p. 105) *[The information in this section of the sentence was a direct quote acquired from the Lavin et al. 2009 publication on page 105.]* and "formal dress led to lower feelings of likeability" "than did casual dress" (Sebastian & Bristow, 2008, p. 200). *[This is a direct quote obtained from Sebastian and Bristow's 2008 publication on page 200.]* Participant answers suggest that students felt more comfortable approaching casually dressed instructors (Carr et al., 2009) *[The information in this section of the sentence was acquired from the Carr et al. 2009 publication.]* as compared to instructors dressed more formally. *[The information in this section of the sentence is my own.]* Generally speaking, the studies have surmised that formal attire generated "enhanced "cool" perceptions" such as: organization skills, knowledge, and preparedness while casual attire produced "better "warm" perceptions" which include: friendliness, flexibility, and sympathy reported by Rollman, (1980) (as cited in Lavin, et al., 2009 p. 4). *[I obtained this information from the Lavin et al 2009 publication, Lavin et al. obtained the information from Rollman's 1980 publication. I included a page number since some of the* *information was directly quoted.]*

Students responded differently along gender lines within the studies; in the Lavin, et al. (2009) research, female respondents viewed formal attire "as somewhat of a negative indication of the instructor's willingness to answer questions and listen to student opinions" (p. 105). "Female students" also perceived "female instructors dressed in casual or business casual attire as more willing to answer questions and listen to student opinions than a female instructor dressed in professional attire" (p.105). Additionally, with this research, male respondents perceived female instructors more negatively than female students' perceived female instructors. As noted earlier in the 'Prior Research' section these findings support past research that suggested, "students may exhibit same gender preferences in their perceptions of faculty" (Lavin, et al., 2009, p. 105). *[The information in this paragraph was obtained from the Lavin et al. 2009 publication on page 105. In the first sentence, I included an in-text citation for a direct quote and included one in the last sentence. I also included page numbers after each direct quote, just to make sure that the reader understands where the information was obtained. I would rather provide too much information for my sources than too little.]*

Limitations. Only one research study provided a definition of 'formal,' 'semi-formal,' and 'casual' clothing. As a result, it is possible that the various studies reached conclusions based on different variables. In the studies researched, only one documented what their target population was while another provided what can be referred to as a disclaimer regarding their target population and their results. *[In these three sentences, I am discussing broad aspects of the studies, this sentence is my creation, no citation required.]* In the Lightstone, et al. (2011) study, research targeted "students taking a second-year accounting course" (p. 19). *[With this sentence, I included part of my in-text citation before the direct quote and the page number* *portion of my in-text citation after the direct quote. This information was obtained from the Lightstone et al. 2011 publication on page 19.]* The Lavin, et al. (2010) study provided the following disclaimer: "the results of this study are based only on data collected at one business school at a small Midwestern university and may not be generalized to broader populations of students" (p. 60). *[This sentence started with the author and year of publication and ended with the page number for the direct quote, the information was obtained from the Lavin et al. 2010 publication on page 60.]* This leads to another limitation of the studies; they were focused on business students exclusively and with the exception of Lightstone et al. (2011), which was conducted in Canada, the studies were conducted in the Mid-Western United States. Two of the surveys were administered at state universities while the other research did not include this information. *[These two sentences are my own, I was discussing the studies in a general sense (overview), and the citation was included since I was referring to the Lightstone et al. 2011 source by name.]*

Lavin et al. (2010) and Sebastian and Bristow's (2008) research were the only two that reported information regarding the gender of the participants. Furthermore, Sebastian and Bristow's (2008) study was the only study to document the participant's average age, despite the fact that this data as well as other demographic information was collected from the respondents. Additionally, many of the studies posed additional questions that were geared towards other research and those results were not shared. In other studies, such as Sebastian and Bristow's (2008) research, instructors' forms of address were also examined. *[This paragraph is my own, again I was discussing the studies in a general sense (overview), and the citations were included since I was referring to the Lavin et al. 2010 and the Sebastian and Bristow (2008) publications by name.]*

Further Research. Research focused on majors other than business and studies conducted in various parts of the country could be implemented. It would also be beneficial if researchers shared more of the demographic information that is collected in their studies. A comparison and possible correlation of student majors, ages, types of schools, and regions of the country could then be implemented. *[This paragraph is my own and I did not refer to any of the studies. Here I provide my opinion in regards to further research on my chosen topic of instructor attire.]*

Conclusion

Studies focused on the impact of college professors' attire on the perceptions of students can be useful to colleges and universities. *[Here I am providing my opinion, no citation required.]* These studies indicated that formal attire "led to greater attributions of expertise than did casual dress" and that "formal dress led to lower feelings of likeability" (Sebastian & Bristow, 2008, p. 200). *[The words in quotation marks were directly quoted from Sebastian and Bristow's 2008 publication on page 200.]* The focus of higher education is student learning. As a result, any factors that may influence student learning should be explored. Additional studies should be conducted that include participants with a variety of student majors, and attending college in various locations throughout the United States. Furthermore, the respondents' demographic information should be shared with these studies in order for correlation and comparisons to be formulated. Is there a correlation between the age (generation), major and type of student (working or not working and full-time or part-time) to their perceptions of their professor's form of attire? Are students' perceptions of their instructor's attire influencing their performance? What other factors that may be influencing perceptions of instructors in addition to attire?

Further research will be conducted involving the correlation between a student's overall perception of their instructor and their final grade. *[These last eight sentences are my opinion, I discussed my views on higher education, future studies, and what questions should be asked in the future; no citation required.]*

References

Carr, D. L., Davies, T. L., & Lavin, A. M. (2009a). The effect of business faculty attire on student perceptions of the quality of instruction and program quality. *College Student Journal, 43*(1), 45-55. Retrieved from http://www.freepatentsonline.com/article/College-Student-Journal/194620722.html.

[Use initials for first and middle names, use a hanging indent (all lines are indented except the first line) ... make sure your information is written in black font, Times New Roman, black, 12-point font, with double-spacing (just like the rest of your paper), no hyperlinks.]

Carr, D. L., Davies, T. L., & Lavin, A. M. (2009b). The male professor's attire and student perceptions of instructional quality. *Research in Higher Education Journal, 4*,1-15. Retrieved from http://www.aabri.com/manuscripts/09254.pdf.

[Regarding "Retrieved from," in APA 6th edition, retrieval dates are only required if the information may change over time, as in the case with wikis (which should not be used in college papers). Additionally, with the first two references, with the year of publication the 'a' with the first source and the 'b' with the second source are present since both sources were written by the same three authors, in the same order (order of contribution) in the same year.]

Carr, D. L., Lavin, A. M & Davies, T.L. (2009). The impact of business faculty attire on student perceptions and engagement. *Journal of College Teaching & Learning, 6*(1), 41-50. Retrieved from http://www.google.com/url?sa=t&rct=j&q=&esrc=s&source=web&cd=1&ved=0ahUKEwiF553X7tXQAhUL6mMKHZ2TDNQQFggaMAA&url=http%3A%2F%2Fcluteinstitute.com%2Fojs%2Findex.php%2FTLC%2Farticle%2Fdownload%2F1180%2F1164&usg=AFQjCNHHG8sCENVVdttA89f27_F9Nvsqeg.

[Do not use databases regarding "Retrieved from," instead use 'doi' numbers. If 'doi' numbers are not available, conduct an internet search and ascertain where the source can be found on the internet and include the url.]

Lavin, A.M., Davies, T. L., & Carr, D. L. (2010). The impact of instructor attire on student perceptions of faculty credibility and their own resultant behavior. *American Journal of Business Education, 3*(6), 51-62. Retrieved from http://files.eric.ed.gov/fulltext/ EJ1058575.pdf

[Book and journals are italicized. With your sources on your reference page, the first word, word after a colon and proper nouns are capitalized. Volume numbers are also italicized, issue numbers are surrounded by parenthesis and are not italicized, neither are page numbers.]

Chickering, A.W., & Gamsom, Z. F., (1987). Seven principles for good practice in undergraduate education. *The Wingspread Journal, 9*(2), Retrieved from https://www.victoria.ac.nz

[With your sources on your reference page, the first word, word after a colon and proper nouns are capitalized, all others should be lower case (sentence-case).]

Franz, M.T., & Norton, S.D., (2001). Investigating business casual dress policies: Questionnaire development and exploratory research. *Applied HRM Research, 6*(2), 79-94. Retrieved from http://www.xavier.edu/appliedhrmresearch/2001-Winter/Franz.pdf.

[Remember to use ampersands (&) with in text citations in parenthesis and your authors on your reference page.]

Lavin, A. M., Carr, D. L., & Davies, T. L. (2009). Does image matter? Female and male student perceptions of the female professor's attire. *Journal of Business and Accounting, 2*(1), 93-106. Retrieved from szethe.files.wordpress.com

Lightstone, K., Francis, R., & Kocum, L. (2011). University faculty style of dress and students'

   perception of instructor credibility. *International Journal of Business & Social Science*,

   2(15), 15-22. Retrieved from http://ijbssnet.com/journals/Vol_2_No_15_August_

   2011/3.pdf

Onwuegbuzie, A.J, Witcher, A.E., Collins, K.M.T., Filer, J.D., Wiedmaier, C.D., & Moore, C.D.

   (2007). Students' perceptions of characteristics of effective college teachers: A validity

   study of a teaching evaluation form using a mixed-methods analysis. *American*

   Educational Journal, 44(1), 113-160. doi: 10.3102/0002831206298169

Sebastian, R. J., & Bristow, D. (2008). Formal or informal? The impact of style of dress and

   forms of address on business students' perceptions of professors. *Journal of Education for*

   Business, *83*(4), 196-201. Retrieved from http://search.proquest.com/openview/4109a01c

   833b3b8f389cfeda646e3537/1?pq-origsite=gscholar

*Explanation details are written after sentences and paragraphs, they will be single spaced,
have 11-point font, and written in Comic Sans.*

The Annotated Bibliography is self-explanatory.

Annotated Bibliography

Title of Article: The Effect of Business Faculty Attire on Student Perceptions of the Quality of Instruction and Program Quality

Reference (APA):	Carr, D.L., Davies, T.L., & Lavin, A.M. (2009a). The effect of business faculty attire on student perceptions of the quality of instruction and program quality. *College Student Journal, 43*(1), 45-55. Retrieved from http://www.freepatentsonline.com/article/College-Student-Journal/194620722.html.
Sample/Population:	Students taking selected business classes in a mid-sized Midwestern university (p. 4) 219 usable "professional" and 227 usable "unprofessional" surveys were collected (p 8).
Purpose:	To assess how a professor's attire and appearance in the classroom might affect student perceptions of the instructor's professionalism and quality of instruction (p. 4).
Question:	Do clothes really make the professor? Does the instructor's clothing choice influence student perceptions of the quality of instruction and educational experience as well as their own ability to find a position and succeed professionally? While prior studies have examined what message is being sent through the academician's choice of clothing, little is known about what impact the professor's attire has on his or her teaching prowess (p. 4).
Procedure/ Methodology/ Study Type questions:	This research is a quantitative, cross-sectional study. Part I consisted of three sections and eighteen questions. First, students were asked how the professor's appearance would influence their perceptions of his or her level of preparation for class, enthusiasm for teaching, knowledge of the subject matter, ability to clearly present information in a understandable way, ability to summarize and emphasize important points, ability to use illustrative examples, ability to introduce stimulating ideas and encourage intellectual effort, concern for student learning, and willingness to answer questions. Second, questions were included as to how the instructor's attire would influence the amount of material being covered, the complexity of the material, and the effective use of class time. Third, students

	were queried as to how the professor's appearance would impact his or her ability to prepare students for a business career as well as the instructor's professionalism, credibility and expertise. Finally, the survey contained two questions on how the professor's usual attire would affect the student's overall evaluation of the course and of the instructor (pp. 4-7).
Findings:	Professional attire and appearance of the instructor does have a positive impact on student perceptions of the instructor, the quality of instruction, the course, and the program (p. 9).
Limitations:	

Title of Article: The Male Professor's Attire and Student Perceptions of Instructional Quality

Reference (APA):	Carr, D.L., Davies, T.L., & Lavin, A.M. (2009b). The male professor's attire and student perceptions of instructional quality. *Research in Higher Education Journal*, 4,1-15. Retrieved from http://www.aabri.com /manuscripts/09254.pdf.
Sample/Population:	Courses were selected from almost all majors offered by the business school including accounting, economics, finance, and management at the undergraduate level as well as from the MBA and MPA (Master of Professional Accountancy) programs. The survey was also administered in several undergraduate mass communications, political science, and psychology classes, as well as two first year law school courses 506 usable responses were obtained. The survey responses were evenly split between male and female, with 265 (52.4%) female respondents and 241 (47.6%) male respondents (p. 5).
Purpose:	To ascertain whether the attire of male professors impacts the perceptions of male and female students differently as to the quality of instruction and their overall satisfaction with the academic program (p. 1).
Procedure/ Methodology:	Male and female students were surveyed using two different versions of a questionnaire which depicted a male model wearing casual, business casual, and professional clothing.
Findings:	In most cases, the male instructor who was dressed more professionally was held in

	higher esteem by students of both genders. However, opposite results were found with respect to the male instructor's ability to relate course information to the real world as well as his willingness to answer questions and listen to student opinions. Further, female students did rate the instructor more positively in all cases, although in some cases the difference was not statistically significant (p. 1).
Limitations:	
Important Points:	Basow and Howe (1982) as well as Ferber and Huber (1975) found that in general female students gave higher ratings than did male students. Basow and Silberg found that male students generally gave female instructors lower ratings as compared to male faculty (1987). In contrast, Bachen et al. (1999) found that male student evaluations did not vary according to the gender of the instructor, but female students gave instructors of their own gender higher ratings as compared to male teachers. Of interest, Basow (1995) found that certain questions resulted in more bias in the responses than did others (p. 3).

Title of Article: The Impact of Business Faculty Attire on Student Perceptions and Engagement

Reference (APA): (Carr, Lavin & Davies 2009)	Carr, D.L., Lavin, A.M & Davies, T.L. (2009). The impact of business faculty attire on student perceptions and engagement. *Journal of College Teaching & Learning, 6*(1), 41-50. Retrieved from journals.cluteo nline.com
Sample/Population:	450 usable surveys, students enrolled in selected business courses at a mid-sized Midwestern university (p. 4).
Purpose:	Explored whether something as basic as the professor's attire could also have a motivating effect on student perceptions and behavior in a college classroom setting.
Question:	"Traditional business dress is seen as a uniform .... It simplifies decision-making and makes hierarchies easy to read." The article concludes with the statement, "The whole idea of dressing for business is to put a

	suit of armor around the body." Would professors also benefit from heeding this advice when it comes to motivating students?
Procedure/ Methodology/ Study Type questions:	Survey questions were patterned after three different student evaluation forms previously or currently being used at the authors' institution, including a form created and used by all general public institutions within the state, the student instructional report II (i.e., SIR II), and the IDEA Diagnostic Form Report. The survey instrument consisted of several sections. Two versions of the survey were administered (pp. 3-4).
Findings:	In general, students perceive professional dress positively, and adjust their behavior accordingly (p. 4).
Limitations:	

Title of Article: The Impact of Instructor Attire on Student Perceptions of Faculty Credibility and their Own Resultant Behavior

Reference (APA): (Lavin, Davies, & Carr, 2010)	Lavin, A.M., Davies, T.L., & Carr, D.L. (2010). The impact of instructor attire on student perceptions of faculty credibility and their own resultant behavior. *American Journal of Business Education*, *3*(6), 51-62. Retrieved from journals.cluteonline.com
Sample/Population:	Students taking select classes at a mid-sized Midwestern university business school were asked to participate/ The genders of the business students who responded were evenly split between female and male, with 216 (47.6%) female respondents and 237 (52.2%) male (p. 5).
Purpose:	To assess how a professor's clothing choice in the classroom might impact their perceptions of the instructor' credibility (p. 3). The purpose of this paper is threefold. The study seeks to determine what instructor traits or characteristics influence student perceptions of the faculty member's credibility. In addition, the project also seeks to determine whether the attire of the faculty member (casual, business causal or professional) influences these perceptions. The authors also attempted to determine how the instructor's perceived attire-dependent

	credibility impacts student effort and behavior (p. 5).
Procedure/ Methodology/ Study Type questions:	Questionnaires depicting instructors of both genders each wearing three different outfits, including casual, business casual and professional attire, are used to assess business student opinions regarding the academician's credibility and the students' resultant effort and learning (p. 3). The survey instrument consisted of several parts including multiple substantive and demographic questions. Students were asked how the professor's various styles of dress would influence their perceptions of the instructor's qualifications and ability to teach, as well as the overall quality of the course, program, and institution (p. 4).
Findings:	The results indicate that faculty members can take comfort in that their level of preparation, knowledge and ability to prepare students for a career do impact their credibility in the eyes of the students, no matter their choice of attire.
Limitations:	
Important Points:	Therefore, the credibility of the faculty member in the eyes of the students does have an impact on the way they act in class as well as their behavior both inside and outside the classroom (p. 9).

Title of Article: Does Image Matter? Female and Male Student Perceptions of the Female Professor's Attire

Reference (APA):	Lavin, A.M., Carr, D.L., & Davies, T.L. (2009). Does image matter? female and male student perceptions of the female professor's attire. *Journal of Business and Accounting*, *2*(1), 93-106. Retrieved from szethe.files. wordpress.com
Sample/Population:	Students taking select classes in a mid-sized Midwestern university (p. 97). Classes chosen included some at the 100 (first year), 200 (second year), 300 (junior level), 400 (senior level) and graduate (700) level. In addition, courses were selected from almost all majors offered by the business school including accounting, finance, and

	management at the undergraduate level as well as from the MBA and MPA (Master of Professional Accountancy) programs, 500 usable responses (p. 99).
Purpose:	The purpose of which was to assess how a female professor's clothing choice in a classroom setting might impact their *(students)* perceptions of the quality of instruction (p. 97).
Question:	Does image matter when it comes to a faculty member's overall classroom performance?
Procedure/ Methodology/ Study Type:	Questionnaire-The first page of the survey was a cover sheet that included three high quality color photos of the same woman instructor wearing three different outfits representing professional, business casual and casual attire (p. 97).
Findings:	Male and female students had a higher opinion of the model female instructor when she was depicted in professional dress versus casual or business casual attire. In only one case were the opposite results true. Specifically, professional dress was viewed as somewhat of a negative indication of the instructor's willingness to answer questions and listen to student opinions, especially with respect to the female students in the sample. The male student responses suggested no significant difference between a female instructor dressed in casual versus business casual or casual versus professional (p. 106).
Limitations:	
Good Points:	Large(r)sample size

Title of Article: University Faculty Style of Dress and Students' Perception of Instructor Credibility

Reference (APA):	Lightstone, K., Francis, R., & Kocum, L. (2011). University faculty style of dress and students' perception of instructor credibility. *International Journal of Business & Social Science, 2*(15), 15-22. Retrieved from http://ijbssnet.com/journals/Vol_2_No_15_August_2011/3.pdf
Sample/Population:	357 Canadian business students
Purpose:	This study focused on what university professors wear and the perceptions of

	students in terms of credibility, character, and likeability (p. 1).
Hypothesis:	*H*1: University professors dressed in formal attire will be perceived by students to have more credibility than professors in casual or semi-formal dress. *H*2: Female university professors will be perceived by students to have less credibility than male university professors (p. 3). The study is also interested in whether university professors' style of dress affects their perceived level of honesty or character and caring or likeability (p. 4).
Procedure/ Methodology/ Study Type:	Survey responding to questions relating to a photograph of a male or female university professor, with faces obscured, and dressed in casual, semi-casual, or formal attire (p. 1).
Variables/Instrumentation/ Definitions:	This study was a true experimental design with individual faculty images randomly assigned to participants. The manipulation, or independent variable, is the image respondents are presented with in terms of style of dress and gender. The dependent variables are the scores on the three scales, credibility, character, and likeability.
Findings:	University professors in formal attire are perceived as more credible than less formally dressed faculty. Contrary to the hypothesis, female formally dressed professors were not perceived as less credible or competent than their male counterparts. Males in formal attire are less likeable than females in formal dress as well as males and females in casual styles of dress (p. 7).
Limitations:	
Promising Related References:	Lavin, Davies, and Carr (2010)

Title of Article: Formal or Informal? The Impact of Style of Dress and Forms of Address on Business Students' Perceptions of Professors

Reference (APA):	Sebastian, R. J., & Bristow, D. (2008). Formal or informal? the impact of style of dress and forms of address on business students' perceptions of professors. *Journal of Education for Business, 83*(4), 196-201. Retrieved from http://search.proquest.com/

	openview/4109a01c833b3b8f389cfeda6 46e3537/1?pq-origsite=gscholar
Sample/Population:	Participants were 103 students (43 women and 60 men) who participated in the first study and 154 students (82 women and 72 men) who participated in the second study. The average age of the participants in both studies was 22 years. Midwestern state universitywere randomly assigned to one of the eight conditions of this study.
Purpose:	To examine the effects of style of dress, forms of address, and gender of the stimulus person on business students' perceptions of professors' attributes.
Research Question:	RQ1: Will formal dress lead to higher levels of perceived instructor trustworthiness? RQ2: Will formal style of address lead to higher levels of perceived instructor trustworthiness? RQ3: Will formal dress lead to higher levels of perceived instructor expertise? RQ4: Will formal style of address lead to higher levels of perceived instructor expertise? RQ5: Will casual dress result in higher levels of instructor attractiveness? RQ6: Will informal style of address result in higher levels of instructor attractiveness RQ7: Will formal dress result in higher levels of instructor credibility? RQ8: Will formal style of address result in higher levels of instructor credibility?
Procedure/ Methodology/ Study Type:	Quantitative, cross-sectional Study: Participants viewed photos and decided between adjectives. The research program consisted of two studies, each featuring three independent variables with two levels of each, resulting in a $2 \times 2 \times 2$ factorial design.
Variables/Instrumentation/ Definitions:	Three independent variables with two levels of each, resulting in a $2 \times 2 \times 2$ factorial design. The independent variables in each study were gender of stimulus person, style of dress (casual or denim shirt and khaki pants, or formal or business suit), and form of address or title (informal or first name or formal or last name) (p. 3).

Findings:	Formal dress led to greater attributions of expertise than did casual dress, whereas formal dress led to lower feelings of likeability on both indexes than did casual dress. It can thus be asserted that either style of dress can be effective, depending on the professor's impression management objectives, in university classrooms. This research indicates that much as other immediately accessible attributes of a professor—such as gender, age, and ethnicity—may create first impressions on students, the professor's style of dress may significantly influence students' impressions of him or her. With this single exception, the procedure and materials for the second study were identical to those for the first study.
Limitations:	
Further Research:	The use of additional stimulus person information and the inclusion of independent variables such as professor approachability, willingness of students to confide in professors, and students' willingness to participate in classroom discussions.
Important Points:	Although one's demographic characteristics are not readily malleable, style of dress is easily manipulated and managed. To this end, professors may want to consider the first impression their style of dress makes on the students in their classrooms (p. 5).
Promising Related References:	Walter, K. (1996, June). Dress for success and comfort. HR Magazine, 41, 55–59.

Chapter 11: An Example of a Literature Review (without comments and explanations, so you can have a visual of what your finished paper should look like)

What a Professor Wears Has an Impact on Student Perceptions

Ronald W. Stephenson II

Wilmington University

What a Professor Wears Has an Impact on Student Perceptions

Introduction

Does a professor's attire have an impact on students' perceptions of their instructor? Ten conclusions can be inferred about a person based exclusively on their attire: "economic level, educational level, trustworthiness, social position, level of sophistication, economic background, social background, educational background, level of success, and moral character" according to Thourlby (1978) (as cited in Lavin, Davies, & Carr, 2009, p. 2). College students may be creating the same conclusions about their professors. If students are generating the same conclusions, this could have an impact on how they perform in class, perceive their professor, and ultimately how students rate their professor on the often-used teacher rating scales. Teacher rating scales are used both formatively and summatively. In the formative sense, these evaluations can help an instructor improve his teaching style and methodology. As a summative tool, the teacher rating scales are used by college administration and may "provide information relevant to promotion, tenure, and pay decisions" (Carr, Davies & Lavin, 2009, p. 52). Consequently, a professor's attire could indirectly effect personnel decisions. Additionally, clothing "influences four kinds of judgments, including credibility, likeability, interpersonal attractiveness, and dominance, and thus serves as a primary impression management tool" as reported by Molloy (1975, 1977) (as cited in Lavin, Carr & Davies, 2009, p. 95). College students may be making these judgments based on an instructor's clothing; if this is the case a professor's attire could have an impact on college instructors' careers.

Organization

This paper includes the following headings: Introduction, Background, Definitions of Attire, Prior Research, Present Research, Conclusion, References, and an Annotated

Bibliography. The Introduction is divided into the subheadings Organization and Inclusion Criteria; Background, which is split into Business World and College Classroom; and the Present Research section is separated into Purpose, Sample, Procedure, Findings, Limitations, and Further Research.

Search Strategy and Inclusion Criteria

The search used for this literature review included EBSCOHost and Google Scholar. The key words were 'correlation between students' perception of their professor and their final grade,' this search resulted in few accessible peer-reviewed articles, as a result, the search was revised into 'student perceptions of their professor's attire.' Within EBSCOHost the following databases were used: Academic Search Premier, Business Source Complete, CINAHL with Full Text, Communication & Mass Media Complete, Computers & Applied Sciences Complete, Education Research Complete, ERIC, Funk & Wagnalls New World Encyclopedia, GreenFILE, Health Source: Nursing/Academic Edition, Humanities International Complete, Library Information Science & Technology Abstracts, MasterFILE Premier, MEDLINE, Middle Search Plus, Primary Search, PsycARTICLES, PsycBOOKS, PsycINFO, Regional Business News, SocINDEX with Full Text, AgeLine, Mental Measurements Yearbook with Tests in Print, and eBook Collection (EBSCOhost).

Background

Business World

Among American organizations, casual dress in the workplace is routine, companies such as IBM and the Ford Motor Company allow casual attire on a daily basis (Sebastian & Bristow, 2008). In the business world, there are many perceived advantages of employees wearing casual clothing. These advantages can be characterized into two domains financial and social. From a financial standpoint, employees save money on the purchase of formal business attire and the elimination of dry-cleaning expenses. Socially, "communication barricades" between leadership and 'general' workers are sometimes lifted as the result of both parties dressing casually (Franz & Norton, 2001, p. 79). Casual dress policies are often viewed as a reward or incentive in many organizations by employees. According to the admittedly "limited survey evidence," casual dress policies in the workplace will lead to improved employee performance (Franz & Norton, 2001, p. 81).

Contrary to the aforementioned information, there is a negative aspect to casual dress in the workplace. Research based on the correlation between people and how they perceive themselves indicates that a person's attire affects their self-perception. People not only "define their roles" by their choice of clothing as reported by Rafaeli, Dutton, Harquail, and Mackie-Lewis (1997) (as cited in Franz & Norton, 2001, p. 81), they also perceive the attributes of their occupation based on the way they dress, according to Kwon (1994b) (as cited in Franz & Norton, 2001). Even though casual dress may have a positive effect on employee attitudes, it could have a detrimental effect on employee performance (Franz & Norton, 2001). Another argument against casual dress in the workplace suggests that employees wearing "formal dress strongly affects how people are treated and that formal codes on dress improve performance, motivation, and attendance" as stated by Molloy (1988) (as cited in Sebastian & Bristow, 2008, p. 196). Additionally, "other writers have suggested that increasing informality is among the causes of the decline in civility of the workplace, where casualness becomes chaos" according to Gonthier (2002) (as cited in Sebastian & Bristow, 2008, p. 197).

College Classroom

According to Lavin, Carr, and Davies (2009) higher education faculty, possibly more than other occupations have substantial discretion regarding their work attire. As a result, what instructors wear at different and the same institutions can vary greatly. What a professor wears is important since college instructors are often perceived as role models to their students.

> Professors
>
> may be serving as an example of what is or is not appropriate in terms of behavior and appearance. Likewise, the extent and even reach of the professor's influence as a knowledge source and mentor may, perhaps, be dependent upon what he wears or at least by how her attire is perceived. (Carr, Davies & Lavin, 2009a, p. 4)

According to Sebastian and Bristow (2008) to students who attend college full time and do not hold jobs, their professors may be one of the few 'professional adult' role models that these students interact with on a regular basis. Aspects of a professor's, demeanor, overall attitude, and attire may provide messages to students. Subsequently, many college students today have full time or part time employment and make the transition from college to the workplace on a day-to-day basis. They may be receiving conflicting messages from work and school; "these students often face either organizational formality or organizational informality" (Sebastian & Bristow, 2008, p. 197).

In higher education, many believe that a professor's principal obligation is to ensure that students "become active participants in their own learning" (Lavin et al., 2009, pp. 93-94). Factors such as appearance may influence a student's desire to learn (Carr et al., 2009a). According to Chickering and Gamson (1987) "learning is not a spectator sport. Students do not learn much just sitting in classes listening to teachers, memorizing pre-packaged assignments, and spitting out answers. They must talk about what they are learning, write about it, relate it to past experiences, and apply it to their daily lives. They must make what they learn part of themselves" (p. 1).

Researchers have proposed that students consider the "following nine characteristics, listed in order of importance" traits of an effective college level educator: "(1) student-centered; (2) knowledgeable about the subject matter; (3) professional; (4) enthusiastic about teaching; (5) effective at communication; (6) accessible; (7) competent at instruction; (8) fair and respectful; and (9) provider of adequate performance feedback described by Witcher et al. (2003), (as cited in Carr et al., 2009a, p. 42). In addition to a professor's attire being related to the overall perception of 'professionalism' that they convey to their students, an instructor's manner of dress correlates with their student's perception of their professor's knowledge and competency.

Definitions of Attire

Recent research defines formal attire for males and females as a "business suit" (Lightsone, Francis & Kocum, 2011, p. 21) or "suits with pants" (Lightsone et al., 2011, p. 18). Semi-formal for the females consisted of a " black shirt dress with leggings and the male in Khakis and a white T-shirt under a blazer" (Lightsone et al., 2011, p.18). Casual dress as a T-shirt and jeans for females and shorts, "a T-shirt, and open long-sleeved button-down shirt for male faculty" (Lightsone et al., 2011, p. 21).

Prior Research

In past studies, it was found that formal attire enhanced "student perceptions of their" instructors' "credibility, intelligence and competence, but" diminished "observed perceptions of likeability and approachability" according to Leathers (1992) (as cited in Lavin et al., 2009, p. 95). Other studies have concluded that professors who "dressed formally were viewed as being more organized, knowledgeable, and better prepared. While those wearing less formal clothing were seen as friendlier, flexible, sympathetic, fair and enthusiastic" as reported by Rollman

(1980) (as cited in Lavin, et al., 2009, p. 95). Prior research has also established that student learning is positively affected by the perceived credibility of the instructor according to Thweatt and McCroskey (1998) (as cited in Lavin, et al., 2009). "Students also tend to recommend credible instructors to others" Nadler and Nadler (2001) reported (as cited in Carr, Lavin & Davies, 2009, p. 52), "respect them," stated Martinez-Egger and Powers (2002) (as cited in Carr et al., 2009, p. 52), "and evaluate them highly" according to Teven and McCroskey (1997) (as cited in Carr et al., 2009, p. 52). Carr et al. (2009) and Sebastian and Bristow (2008) discovered that students ascribe more expertise to instructors who are formally dressed as compared to their casually dressed peers. Consequently, formally dressed professors were rated lower regarding likeability (Carr et al., 2009; Sebastian & Bristow, 2008).

Prior research has also established a possible gender bias, it seems as though students may display "same gender preferences in their perceptions" of college instructors (Lavin et al., 2009, p. 105). It was also established that regarding teacher ratings "female students gave higher ratings" than "did male students" reported Basow and Howe (1982) and Ferber and Huber (1975) (as cited in Carr, Davies, & Lavin 2009b, p. 3) and "that male students generally gave female instructors lower ratings as compared to male faculty" described by Basow and Silberg, (1987) (as cited in Carr et al., 2009b, p. 3). "In contrast, male student evaluations did not vary according to the gender of the instructor, but female students gave instructors of their own gender higher ratings as compared to male teachers" according to Bachen et al. (1999) as (as cited in Carr et al., 2009b, p. 3).

Present Research

Purpose

The purpose of the studies was to determine how professors' clothing effects student perceptions about a professor's credibility and professionalism (Lavin, et al., 2009). The general

hypothesis among the studies was that formal attire would lead to enhanced perceptions of

expertise and credibility with decreased perceptions of likeability and openness (Lightstone, et

al., 2011; Sebastian & Bristow 2008). There were a few variations regarding gender within the

studies; the studies researched were mainly exploring both male and female instructor's attire

with two exceptions. Carr et al., (2009) examined the perceptions of females only while Carr et

al., (2009b) was limited to male professors.

Samples. Non-random, purposeful, voluntary sampling was employed with the studies

explored. Non-random and purposeful since specific college classes were identified and the

sample was voluntary since as previously discussed within the "Procedure" section, the

completion of the survey was optional. For the most part, the studies' participants were business

students from mid-sized Midwestern universities with the exception being the Lightstone, et al.

(2011) research that was conducted at a Canadian university. The Lightstone, et al. (2011)

research was also the exception regarding the major of the participants, this study included

business as well as psychology students. Additionally, the Carr et al. (2009b) study included

"MBA and MPA (Master of Professional Accountancy) programs" and "several undergraduate

mass communication, political science," "psychology classes," and "two first year law school

courses" (p. 5). The mean number of participants in the studies was 388 and the median was

450. The fewest participants were 103 while the largest number was 506.

The gender of the participants was discussed in two of the studies; Sebastian and

Bristow's (2008) and Carr, Davies, and Lavin's (2010) study. In Sebastian and Bristow's (2008)

research, there were "103 students (43 women and 60 men)" in the first study and "154 students

(82 women and 72 men) who participated in the second study" (p. 198). In the Carr et al. (2010)

study, participants "were fairly evenly split between female and male, with 216 (47.6%) female respondents and 237 (52.2%) male respondents" (p. 51).

Procedures. In three out of the seven studies, participants were provided with photographs of faculty members dressed in various forms of clothing while the remaining studies provided written descriptions of the professor's attire being examined. The participants were then asked questions about each faculty member via a written survey (Lavin et al., 2009). One of the studies contained an on-line aspect that did not differentiate from the "traditional" survey except in its delivery mode (Lightstone et al., 2011). The only other difference (however slight) in survey delivery that was noted within the studies was Sebastian and Bristow (2008) "who seated the participants" in a theater style room that contained a large screen projection system and folding desks for writing (p. 198). It can be inferred that the other studies that were "traditional" in delivery were administered in college classrooms.

All the studies reviewed were quantitative and cross-sectional in nature. Students answered the questions by providing a numerical value to their answers as exemplified in the Lavin et al. (2009) research. Respondents ranked how "a professor's attire would impact their perception of the instructor, where 1 = significantly positive, 2 = somewhat positive, 3 = no difference, 4 = somewhat negative, and 5 = significantly negative" (p. 6). As mentioned previously, the lone difference was Sebastian and Bristow (2008) who employed a choice between adjectives. Furthermore, data were collected at one point in time.

Two different versions of a study were utilized in three of the studies researched. In the Lavin et al. 2009 study, two different versions of their survey were used "to change the order in which the" (p. 98) photographs of the instructor's "clothing was presented. In one case the instructor was depicted wearing casual, business casual, and professional dress (Version 1) respectively, while in the second version the same instructor was depicted wearing professional, business casual and casual clothing (Version 2)" (p. 98). In Sebastian and Bristow's (2008) research two surveys were used although it was unclear the reason for this. This research was not only examining the impact of instructors' attire on student perceptions but also the impact of instructor's form of address on student perceptions of their professor. The additional survey may have focused primarily on the forms of address aspect of the research. In the Carr et al. (2009a) research, two different versions of their study were employed as well; "one version asked students to assume the professor's attire and appearance was professional while the alternative assumed unprofessional dress" (p. 7).

Another variation of the procedure in which the studies were implemented was Sebastian and Bristow's (2008) research where there was a screen in front of the classroom and participants were instructed to view a description of the instructor that corresponded with the photograph the respondents were viewing. Additionally, this survey asked the participants to "rate the stimulus persons on 18 trait adjective pairs" (p. 198). This research

used the 15-item scale developed by Ohanian (1990) to measure the attractiveness (unattractive or attractive, not classy or classy, ugly or beautiful, plain or elegant, not sexy or sexy), trustworthiness (undependable or dependable, dishonest or honest, unreliable or reliable, insincere or sincere, untrustworthy or trustworthy), and expertise (not an expert or expert, inexperienced or experienced, unknowledgeable or knowledgeable, unqualified or qualified, unskilled or skilled). (p. 198).

The other studies examined asked questions such as:

The level of the instructors' preparation for class.

The instructor's knowledge of the material (i.e., subject matter).

The instructor's ability to present information clearly and in an understandable manner.

The student's overall evaluation of the instructor.

The reputation of the institution.

The value of the educational experience. (Lavin, et al., 2009, p. 98).

Regarding the studies where questions were asked, half of these studies included questions that were divided into categories while the other studies consisted of a single list of questions. The categories of questions amongst the studies were "how the instructor's attire would influence their overall appreciation for the course," "how the professor's appearance would impact their own engagement in the classroom," and "how the professor's appearance might affect their own engagement outside the classroom" (Carr, et al., 2009, p. 43). Other categories were "Instructor Characteristics that May Impact Credibility," "Instructor Credibility," "Student Effort and Behavior" (Lavin, et al., 2010, p. 54) "credibility, character, and likeability measures" (Lightstone, et al., 2011, p. 19). The aforementioned questions and categories of questions were referring to either a photograph or a written description of instructors dressed in formal, semi-formal, or in casual attire. Many of the questions were influenced by existing evaluations at the researchers' institution (Lavin et al., 2009).

A consistent theme throughout the studies was that the participants were informed that the professors' manner of dress was a personal preference and factors such as: "classroom conditions (e.g., heating, cooling and ventilation), the class setting (e.g., evening class, length of class session), delivery mode (e.g., face to face versus distance) and his or her individual preferences and comfort" (Carr et al., 2009b, p. 4) should be taken into account. Additionally, students were notified that the studies were not intended to be an appraisal of any specific instructor and formal dress codes did not exist at the colleges where the studies took place (Carr et al., 2010). It can be inferred that all the participants of the studies examined were informed that the surveys were optional and the results confidential. One study included an extra credit incentive for its participants (Lightstone, et al., 2011). Another theme throughout the studies was the participants reporting of their demographic information.

Findings. Professors wearing formal attire were perceived as being "more credible" (Lightstone, et. al., 2011, p. 7) and formal attire "led to greater attributions of expertise than did casual dress" (Sebastian & Bristow, 2008, p. 200). Conversely, formal attire was perceived as a weakness in regards to an "instructor's willingness to answer questions and listen to student opinions" (Lavin et al., 2009, p. 105) and "formal dress led to lower feelings of likeability" "than did casual dress" (Sebastian & Bristow, 2008, p. 200). Participant answers suggest that students felt more comfortable approaching casually dressed instructors (Carr et al., 2009) as compared to instructors dressed more formally. Generally speaking, the studies have surmised that formal attire generated "enhanced "cool" perceptions" such as: organization skills, knowledge, and preparedness while casual attire produced "better "warm" perceptions" which include: friendliness, flexibility, and sympathy reported by Rollman, (1980) (as cited in Lavin, et al., 2009, p. 4).

Students responded differently along gender lines within the studies; in the Lavin, et al. 2009 research female respondents viewed formal attire "as somewhat of a negative indication of the instructor's willingness to answer questions and listen to student opinions" (p. 105). "Female students" also perceived "female instructors dressed in casual or business casual attire as more willing to answer questions and listen to student opinions than a female instructor dressed in professional attire" (p. 105). Additionally, with this research, male respondents perceived female instructors more negatively than female students' perceived female instructors. As noted earlier in the 'Prior Research' section these findings support past research that suggested, "students may exhibit same gender preferences in their perceptions of faculty" (Lavin, et al., 2009, p. 105).

Limitations. Only one research study provided a definition of 'formal,' 'semi-formal,' and 'casual' clothing. As a result, it is possible that the various studies reached conclusions based on different variables. In the studies researched only one documented what their target population was while another provided what can be referred to as a disclaimer regarding their target population and their results. With the Lightstone, et al. (2011) study, research targeted "students taking a second-year accounting course" (p. 19). The Lavin et al. (2010) study provided the following disclaimer: "the results of this study are based only on data collected at one business school at a small Midwestern university and may not be generalized to broader populations of students" (p. 60). This leads to another limitation of the studies; they were focused on business students exclusively and with the exception of Lightstone et al. (2011), which was conducted in Canada, the studies were conducted in the Mid-Western United States. Two of the surveys were administered at state universities while the other research did not include this information.

Lavin et al. (2010) and Sebastian and Bristow's (2008) research were the only two that reported information regarding the gender of the participants. Furthermore, Sebastian and Bristow's (2008) study was the only study to document the participant's average age, despite the fact that this data as well as other demographic information was collected from the respondents. Additionally, many of the studies posed additional questions that were geared towards other research and those results were not shared. In other studies, such as Sebastian and Bristow's (2008) research, instructors' forms of address were also examined.

Further Research. Research focused on majors other than business and studies conducted in various parts of the country could be implemented. It would also be beneficial if researchers shared more of the demographic information that is collected in their studies. A comparison and possible correlation of student majors, ages, types of schools, and regions of the country could then be implemented.

Conclusion

Studies focused on the impact of college professors' attire on the perceptions of students can be useful to colleges and universities. These studies indicated that formal attire "led to greater attributions of expertise than did casual dress" and that "formal dress led to lower feelings of likeability" (Sebastian & Bristow, 2008, p. 200). The focus of higher education is student learning. As a result, any factors that may influence student learning should be explored. Additional studies should be conducted that include participants with a variety of student majors, and attending college in various locations throughout the United States. Furthermore, the respondents' demographic information should be shared with these studies in order for correlation and comparisons to be formulated. Is there a correlation between the age (generation), major and type of student (working or not working and full-time or part-time) to their perceptions of their professor's form of attire? Are students' perceptions of their instructor's attire influencing their performance? What other factors that may be influencing perceptions of instructors in addition to attire? Further research will be conducted involving the correlation between a student's overall perception of their instructor and their final grade.

References

Carr, D. L., Davies, T. L., & Lavin, A. M. (2009a). The effect of business faculty attire on student perceptions of the quality of instruction and program quality. *College Student Journal*, *43*(1), 45-55. Retrieved from http://www.freepatentsonline.com/article/College-Student-Journal/194620722.html.

Carr, D. L., Davies, T. L., & Lavin, A. M. (2009b). The male professor's attire and student perceptions of instructional quality. *Research in Higher Education Journal*, *4*,1-15. Retrieved from http://www.aabri.com/manuscripts/09254.pdf.

Carr, D. L., Lavin, A. M & Davies, T.L. (2009). The impact of business faculty attire on student perceptions and engagement. *Journal of College Teaching & Learning, 6*(1), 41-50. Retrieved from http://www.google.com/url?sa=t&rct=j&q=&esrc=s&source=web&cd=1&ved=0ahUKEwiF553X7tXQAhUL6mMKHZ2TDNQQFggaMAA&url=http%3A%2F%2Fcluteinstitute.com%2Fojs%2Findex.php%2FTLC%2Farticle%2Fdownload%2F1180%2F1164&usg=AFQjCNHHG8sCENVVdttA89f27_F9Nvsqeg.

Lavin, A.M., Davies, T. L., & Carr, D. L. (2010). The impact of instructor attire on student perceptions of faculty credibility and their own resultant behavior. *American Journal of Business Education*, *3*(6), 51-62. Retrieved from http://files.eric.ed.gov/fulltext/EJ1058575.pdf

Chickering, A.W., & Gamsom, Z. F., (1987). Seven principles for good practice in undergraduate education. *The Wingspread Journal*, *9*(2)*,* Retrieved from https://www.victoria.ac.nz

Franz, M.T., & Norton, S.D., (2001). Investigating business casual dress policies: Questionnaire development and exploratory research. *Applied HRM Research, 6*(2), 79-94. Retrieved from http://www.xavier.edu/appliedhrmresearch/2001-Winter/Franz.pdf.

Lavin, A. M., Carr, D. L., & Davies, T. L. (2009). Does image matter? Female and male student perceptions of the female professor's attire. *Journal of Business and Accounting, 2*(1), 93-106. Retrieved from szethe.files.wordpress.com

Lightstone, K., Francis, R., & Kocum, L. (2011). University faculty style of dress and students' perception of instructor credibility. *International Journal of Business & Social Science, 2*(15), 15-22. Retrieved from http://ijbssnet.com/journals/Vol_2_No_15_August_ 2011/3.pdf

Onwuegbuzie, A.J, Witcher, A.E., Collins, K.M.T., Filer, J.D., Wiedmaier, C.D., & Moore, C.D. (2007). Students' perceptions of characteristics of effective college teachers: A validity study of a teaching evaluation form using a mixed-methods analysis. *American Educational Journal, 44*(1), 113-160. doi: 10.3102/0002831206298169

Sebastian, R. J., & Bristow, D. (2008). Formal or informal? The impact of style of dress and forms of address on business students' perceptions of professors. *Journal of Education for Business, 83*(4), 196-201. Retrieved from http://search.proquest.com/openview/4109a01c 833b3b8f389cfeda646e3537/1?pq-origsite=gscholar

Appendix: Feel Free to Copy the Appendix and use it as a checklist. Please only copy what you need or save this as a Word Document and reuse. Let's save the trees!

(The Appendix are Chapters 1, 2 & 3 {the "How to" directions} in list format)

Appendix A

How to Write Research Papers

Day 1: **Choose** a topic that you are interested in (if possible).

Then thoroughly read the **assignment directions** and the **rubric**.

Day 2: **Search** the Library, EBSCO Host, Google Scholar, and Google. **Always back up your work!**

Make sure you save the name and site where you obtained your articles (so you can quickly go back to them in case they get lost or your computer freezes). *Even if you do not re-write an author's information word for word, an in-text citation and corresponding Reference page citation is required.*

Day 3: **Briefly** read the articles or other information to make sure that they will fit into your paper.

With the articles that fit, make sure you create the appropriate corresponding citation (APA or MLA).

Day 4: **Outline**, divide your topic into an introduction, at least three subtopics, and a conclusion.

Then document which article should go with which section of your paper.

Day 5: **Start Writing**, pay close attention to what information was obtained from what source.

Highlight information that is not your own and keep it highlighted until you have created the appropriate in text citation.

Day 6: **Continue** to write or **reread** and **proofread** your paper and then write your conclusion.

After your conclusion is finished, have it proofread by a reliable person.

Day 7: **Correspond** with your proofreader, make changes, reread your paper and then submit.

Appendix B

How to Write Article Summaries

Day 1: **Read** the entire article.

Day 2: **Read** the **assignment directions** and the **rubric. Always back up your work!**

Highlight the assignment directions in various colors.

Copy the entire article and paste it as a Microsoft Word Document. ***Make sure you properly cite the article***. Place the required citation (APA/ MLA, or other) at the top of your word document. **Always make sure you provide proper credit to your sources**. *You are only transferring the author's words onto a Word document so you can highlight them in the various colors that Word provides.*

As you read the article again highlight the various sections in the color that correspond with the assignment directions that you will be answering with the information highlighted.

Never write an author's words directly into your paper unless you provide the proper citation as a direct quote (author, year of publication, page, paragraph, or section number). Remember, directly quoting an author's information is fine if you provide the proper citations and you do this sparingly. *Even if you do not re-write an author's information word for word, an in-text citation and corresponding Reference page citation is required.*

Day 3: **Outline** by dividing your topic into an introduction, at least three subtopics, and a conclusion.

Then document which piece of information should go with which section of your paper.

Day 4: **Read the Rubric again,** then start writing, pay close attention to what information was obtained from what source.

Highlight information that is not your own and keep it highlighted until you have created the appropriate in text citation.

Day 5: **Continue** to write or **reread** and **proofread** your paper and then write your conclusion.

After your conclusion is finished, have your paper proofread by a reliable person.

Day 6: **Correspond** with your proofreader, make changes, reread your paper and then submit.

Appendix C

How to Write Other University Level Assignments

Day 1: **Read** the assignment directions and the rubric.

Highlight the assignment directions in various colors.

If possible, copy the information required for your assignment and paste it in a Microsoft Word Document. Make sure you properly cite the information. Place the required citation at the top of your word document. ***Always make sure you provide proper credit to your sources.* You are only transferring the author's words onto a Word document so you can highlight them in the various colors that Word provides.**

As you read the information again, highlight the various sections in the color that correspond with the assignment directions/ rubric sections that you will be answering with the information highlighted. Never write an author's words directly into your paper unless you provide the proper citation as a direct quote (author, year of publication, page number).

Remember, directly quoting an author's information is fine if you provide the proper citations and you do this sparingly.

Day 2: **Briefly re-read** the information that needs to be included within your paper. **Always back up your work!**

With this information, make sure you create the appropriate corresponding (APA/MLA or other) citation. *Even if you do not re-write an author's information word for word, an in-text citation and corresponding Reference page citation is required.*

Day 3: **Outline** by dividing your topic into an introduction, at least three subtopics, and a conclusion.

Then document which article should go with which section of your paper.

Day 4: **Start writing**, make sure you pay close attention as to what information was obtained from what source.

Highlight information that is not your own and keep it highlighted until you have created the appropriate in text citation.

Day 5: **Continue** to write or **reread** and **proofread** your paper and then write your conclusion.

After your conclusion is finished, have your paper proofread by a reliable person.

Day 6: **Correspond** with your proofreader, make changes, reread your paper and then submit.

Acknowledgements

Thanks to my wife Nygai who endured me earning three out of my four degrees (I wasn't married during my undergraduate years) and writing too many papers!

Thanks to my mother Cassandra A. Stephenson who proofread all those papers. After all of that she is still editing my work!

Thanks to my children Ronald III, Robert, Xavier and my dog Timber who had no choice but to put up with me while I was writing.

Thanks to my friends and family who showed patience, (I had to miss a few family and friend gatherings to write those papers).

Thanks

Thanks to the Publication Manual of the American Psychological Association 6th Edition. I used the manual extensively as a student, I continue to review the manual as a professor (to make sure I am correct when grading and advising students). As an author and behavioral scientist, I continue to use the manual. I referred to the Publication Manual of the American Psychological Association 6th Edition while writing this book to ensure that I was correct.

Remember, regardless of what I wrote regarding APA, the manual wins!

Special Thanks

A special thanks to Rex Chege, Brittany E. Currington, Diamond Ridgeway, Cory L. Sullivan Jr., and Ronald W. Stephenson III. My first book reading focus group. It took me nearly a month to review your comments with the help of III; even though I have a bunch of degrees and have been a teacher and professor for many years, not the easiest thing to hear critiques. I guess I need to get used to this, after all I am an author now! I want you to know that your comments and suggestions were invaluable. I appreciate your honest opinions. Come over anytime for more pizza!

Special Acknowledgement

Thanks to Doctors Johanna Bishop and Stephanie Berridge. Dr. Bishop, you have been an excellent role model and mentor since you hired me over eight years ago. Dr. Berridge, I continue to appreciate your feedback and honest assessments. I learned a lot from the two of you regarding grammar, mechanics, word usage, APA, and general writing/ grading guidelines. Thanks again for your continued support. Additionally, I want to thank the instructor of my most challenging doctoral courses, Dr. Lynne Svenning. Dr. Svenning, I learned a great deal about APA and writing from the feedback you provided on my assignments.

Afterword

Thank you for reading, I hope this quick guide helps. If you enjoyed this quick read, you may also like *Reflections from a Graduate Student* in which I discuss my experience in grad school. This book should be available later this year in 2017. If you are interested in autism, especially autism diagnosis, my first book *The Disparities of Autism Diagnosis within the United States* which is actually my dissertation that various journals did not want to publish (long story) is available.

Remember, grades are not given, they are earned!

Made in the USA
Middletown, DE
08 August 2023

36404769R00043